JOURNEYS OF
Faith and *Love*

JOURNEYS OF
Faith and *Love*

JOHNNY BROWN

authorHOUSE®

AuthorHouse™
1663 Liberty Drive
Bloomington, IN 47403
www.authorhouse.com
Phone: 1-800-839-8640

Published by AuthorHouse   06/29/2012

ISBN: 978-1-4772-1084-0 (sc)
ISBN: 978-1-4772-1083-3 (e)

Library of Congress Control Number: 2012909360

Any people depicted in stock imagery provided by Thinkstock are models, and such images are being used for illustrative purposes only.
Certain stock imagery © Thinkstock.

This book is printed on acid-free paper.

Because of the dynamic nature of the Internet, any web addresses or links contained in this book may have changed since publication and may no longer be valid. The views expressed in this work are solely those of the author and do not necessarily reflect the views of the publisher, and the publisher hereby disclaims any responsibility for them.

Dedication

This book is dedicated to my grandma Noni. Ever since I was a kid you have been special to me. Nothing can replace the joy and the memories of watching the Giants win the World Series with you. I thank God for that opportunity and the many opportunities that I have had to spend time with you, cause as life goes on I don't know how many more days I have with you. I will always love you and always think of you before I do anything.

Thank you:

Mom and Bob: Mom you always had my best interests in mind no matter what anybody said or what their opinions were. Though, we don't always agree and I follow my own path I will always love you and watch my things. I love you mom.

Dad and Debbie: You guys have always given me the freedom to live my life, but have always been there for me. I don't know how you guys know when to say just what I need to hear when I need to hear it, but somehow you do. I love you both.

Jess, CJ, Kyle, Tiff, & Brooke: You guys are source of great joy for me, I love you all and I am always there for you no matter what. I am just a phone call away.

Mark & Agg. Shell & JJ: Thank you for everything you all have done and the love you have shown me. I love you all.

Jill: You are a strong woman. Thank you for being a friend

Tears: Thank you for all the times I needed someone to put me in my place, thank you for being that friend.

Sigma Nu: For all my friends that I have met and still to this day spend time with, you all have, in many ways, inspired me to follow my dreams. You guys will always be special to me. Thank you.

But Tonight
―――∞∞∞―――

At times now when I close my eyes
I stray back to different times
I do not wish to be in those situations again
For destiny cannot be changed
I do not regret
I just wish for another whiff of that sweet scent
To feel strands of silk cover my body
To run my hands over smooth curves
To explore every inch
But like the hands of time
They just push relentlessly forward
I cannot go back
But tonight
I don't want to be anywhere but here with you
You have my complete attention
I will do nothing but please you in every way
My mind will not stray
I will explore every inch
Tonight I will take my time
I will not rush,
I will enjoy every minute
But tonight I will . . . .

Weary

Father my shoulders are weary from the heavy burden that has been laid upon them

My legs are weary from trudging through the mud that I have been going through

I am tired, for I have not had a chance to rest

Let me lean against you, so my legs wont buckle again

Take this burden from my shoulders so I can regain my strength

Allow my head to rest against your shoulder, so I can get some peace

When I am finally strong, and I can withstand the storms that may come my way

Don't walk a head of me, for I do not want to lose sight of you

Don't walk behind me, because I don't want to go before you

Walk next to me so that I know you will always be there

Crying In Bed Next To You

As I lay in bed next to you I hold back the tears that want
To fall like heavy rain drops during a storm
I don't want to show that I am weak
As I lay next to you
Those words that fall upon my ears like drops of acid upon metal
I don't want to show you that I can't take it
So those tears you will never see
The times that we make love
Are like a beautiful interlude to what may come
Those times that I hold you so close, so warm, so tight
I want it to last all through the night
But alas our bodies can't last forever
As we lay there I hear those words that cause these tears
I have so many fears
As you fall asleep
I lay silently next to you
Trying to hold back the deluge of tears
But the tears fall down like rain, but I don't make a sound
As I am lying in bed crying next to you

Don't Know What To Say, Don't know What To Do

When all the words have been said and I don't know what to say
Even when speaking from my heart, I am still speechless
I will just be here loving you
When I can't see you, touch you, hold you
And I am frustrated because I don't know what to do
I will still be here loving you
I have told you all that I could
I said everything from my heart
My mind can't find another word
But the only thing I can do is stay here and love you
I have tried to go on but somehow, some way
I come back to loving you
Weather I watch you walk away or hear of another
And the pain of that is unbearable
I will still be here loving you
Loving you is what I do
Because I don't know what to say, I don't know what to do

Here I Stand
───❦───

Here I stand in front a woman
Trying to be a rock and play the role
Here I stand in front a woman
Saying my shoulder is yours
Here I stand hoping wishing
Just a man trying to be the one
Just a man making mistakes, hoping I can be forgiven
In reality
I am just a boy standing on wobbly knees
Shaking
In front of girl asking a girl
To go out with him

How You Make Me Feel

You make me smile when I hear your voice
My heart pounds like the first time a boy calls a girl

I see you constantly in my dreams
I feel your body next to mine as I sleep
You are with me wherever I go

You are my first thought as well as my last thought
I can't wait until the next time we talk
All these words just to say three simple ones

. . . I LOVE YOU . . .

I Adored You

There were times, when you cared if I adored you
We shared times, just you and I
It didn't matter what you were doing, time didn't go by without you
thinking of me, as I always thought of you
We laughed and had quite times
Now I wonder where you went
Now I wonder if you even care
I thought you cared if I adored you
But now it would seem that you care more that the
World adores you
It would seem that I have been cast aside without a thought
If you assume that I went away, like times before
I haven't.
I stood aside cause it seemed you cared more about the world adoring
you
Than the fact that I adored you.

Chasing Ghosts

Sometimes we surrender to pretty eyes
In truth all we do is surrender to their lies
That perfect body we just want to hold close
But yet all we do is hold air
Even the beauty of their hair
We think are strands of gold
Their voice is like angels singing
At first it's like heaven
Then we wonder why it ends the way it does
We give love so freely
Yet receive none in return
At times we need a rock to help support a weary body
But we end up falling when there is nothing to support us
So why do we end up chasing ghosts

I Can Hear Your Heart

I can hear your heart
No I don't have to have my ear upon your chest
Nor do I have to be next to you
At times it is like a gentle breeze washing over my ears
But now it's like a mighty wind, powerful and strong
It calls for me, not to save
Not to help
But to listen
Yearning to be heard to be free
Wanting to be held again in strong hands
To be loved again to take away all the pain
To take away all the confusion
I can hear your heart
Wanting to take over instead of following your mind
Instead of blindly following where your feet lead
It doesn't reach out, it does not cry yet
I can hear your heart
Telling, yelling, wishing, seeking
To be free again, to be free of what holds it down
Like a prisoner that has no chance
Wanting to rise up out of the chains that weigh it down
I can hear your heart

How did we get here

How did we get from smiles and laughter
To tears and frowns
It wasn't that long ago that we shared smiles
It was that long ago when we talked well into the morning light
But how did we get here
When there is more silence than talk
Maybe we didn't start the way we should
Maybe I didn't say or do the things I should have
But how did we get here
Life does change, we get busy, we have goals to pursue
But how did we get to here
I look back when stupid grins couldn't be removed
When feet were lighter and steps were together
I close my eyes hoping to be in a dream
But when slumber doesn't overtake, I ask how did we get here

I Close My Eyes

I close my eyes I can still see your smile
As beautiful as the sunrise
I close my eyes when I go to sleep
I can still see your body next to me
Your back is to me, the curves of your hips, the shape of your back
All imprinted on my mind
I reach out and can feel your velvet soft skin
I feel your back how warm it is,
The way my hand glides like a gentle breeze over your body, feeling you
close to me
I close my eyes and still feel your hair as it falls over me when you lay on me
The softness of each strand like strands of silk
The kisses are still upon my lips
I close my eyes and you are there with me
Holding, touching . . . . loving

Just A Spot

Sometimes as I make my way around
I ride by places that to others are just spaces or spots
Nothing more, nothing less
Though I see picture perfect times
Where God has stopped time and I can see
There is where I held you so close, but only for the night
Here is where we stopped while it poured
Here is where we kissed the night away
That feeling will stray
There is where we watched the sunset and our hopes rose
Here is where we could see far and wide
There nothing could hide
Now as time marches on
It becomes
Just a spot

I Dream Of You

I often dream of you
Skin so soft
I like how you feel when you're next to me

I often dream of you
Your touch so gentle
I relax when you lay your hands upon me

I often dream of you
Getting lost in your eyes
And not wanting to be found

I often dream of you
Holding you close to me until the morning light

I often dream of you
Kissing you, caressing you, holding you

Knocking on your door . . . .

I sit like a kid in front of a door
A rose in hand
Knocking on your door
Hoping with every second that goes by
That you will answer it
Wanting to be next to you
Wanting to wrap my arms around you
Waiting for that next time to see you
With the passing of every second seems like
A season has passed
Hoping that this wont be the last I knock at your door
So until you open your door
Here I stand hoping, waiting . . . .

I Drew A Heart In The Sand

I drew a heart in the sand
Hoping it would last
Alas a wave came and washed it away
I hoped that wouldn't be us
Happy I got to hold you close
To walk in hand in hand
To be able to gaze into your eyes
And be close to you
Sad that it had to end the way it did
Sad that it didn't last
But at least I drew a heart in the sand

Heaven

You got me on my knees praying
And saying please let this be
True sight unseen
Yet my ears see everything that my eyes cannot
You got me wanting to sleep quick so I can wake up just to hear your
voice
Touch unfelt, but yet when I close my eyes I touch you with my heart
Do I fall quickly, no strength holds, but even a redwood can fall
I live for that moment when laughter is the sound that I hear,
I want to stay there listening to your every breath, awaiting every word
not because we are bored and there is nothing left to say
But because I know these times when it feels so good, when just listening
Is some how just perfect
But these feelings and these times, before now are but only a few,
If you could place value it would be priceless
So rare it is, it's like a weary man just falling down upon a soft bed
He knows he has to get up at some point, but for those few moments
He is in heaven

I Should Have

I should have held you closer to me
Instead somebody is holding you tonight by the moon light
I should have told you that I love you more
Instead of not saying anything
I should have bit my tongue more
And those words would have never been said
I should have kissed you more
Instead of just leaving you alone
I should have enjoyed those silly moments instead of being rigid
I should have smiled more instead of frowning
I should have made love to you more, instead of being mad
I should have held hands instead of walking a head
I should have been more patient instead of being impatient
I should have saw all instead of being short sighted
I should have, but I didn't . . . . that's why you are there and not here

I Didn't Want To Miss You Like This

I didn't want to miss you like this
With every step that takes me away from you
I think of what may have been, even what could have been
No matter where I am, I wish you were next to me
Even when there are people around I feel alone
Wishing I had you next to me
I keep my head up saying that if it meant anything then
It would have been something
That still doesn't change that I still miss you
When I lay myself down to sleep
And I close my eyes, there are times I feel
Like I am reaching out to you, trying to grasp you and hold on
I miss your touch and your kiss
I miss your laugh and walk
I miss watching you dance, wishing that I could be out there
With you dancing with you
Damn this feeling that I have
Thinking I was right, though I may have been wrong
In the end it doesn't matter
Cause it brings the same thing
Me alone
I never thought that I was going to feel this way
I never thought I would think this way
Because I didn't want to miss you like this

I Tell Myself

———∞∞∞———

I try and tell myself if you left now I wouldn't care
It just started there can't be any feelings to spare
Butt tell me how to forget about somebody with a voice like an angel
Tell me how to forget about lips like velvet when pressed against mine
Tell me how to forget about your touch, your kiss, the way you feel in
my arms
If you tell my mind to forget, it will
But if you tell my heart to do the same, it may only for a day
But only for a day, how can I forget about someone special, but even
more rare
It wouldn't dare

I Go Back

Though I say to myself that this life I have chosen is fine
That this path that I follow is wise
That being alone is bittersweet
Those many days left behind are like a gentle breeze washing over me on
a hot day
During the day I do not allow myself to embrace what my mind reflects
upon
At night, before I slumber is when I allow these feelings to wash over me
I do not reflect upon words that were meant to tear down
I do not recall actions that, weather right or wrong, have led me down
this way
No at night before I slumber, alone
That is when I close my eyes,
That is when I can feel that sweet, warmth embrace that only lovers
share
I will feel this way again but for now I go back
To when long warm kisses fell upon my lips, like rain quenching the
driest field
I go back to days of laughter, when laughter rang more true than the
silence
That pervades these ears now
I go back to looks of longing, that only lovers share
That now, are like a perfect stone, very rare
I go back to perfect nights, when I can still feel silky smooth skin
Underneath my finger tips as I trace my fingers upon a bare back

I can feel the goose bumps rise and fall with every slight touch
I go back to when strands of hair fell upon my chest,
I can feel every soft strand,
I will feel this way again, for now I go back.

Times Spent

As the rain falls

I sit back and recall

The days spent with you during the fall

Now as I listen to the thunder I wonder

If we can be together again

You are a godsend

The nights spent under the stars

Were the best by far

But as our paths go parallel

Do I say farewell

Or open my arms for you again

I Hoped it was you

Last night I heard my phone ring, I hoped it was you as I picked it up
Sadly the voice on the other end was not yours
A car pulled up next to me at the light, that looked like yours
But the driver was not you
I thought I saw you in the gym
But as the person turned around it was not you
The door bell rang and I went to open it . . . .
I hoped it was you . . . .

I Wanna Be There

As you walk down the path of life I wanna be there hand in hand
When laughter rings I wanna be there to laugh with you
As life's burdens hold you down
And the weight is too much to bare, I wanna be there to hold you up
As you lay your head down, I wanna be there so that you can rest your
head upon me
When generations surround you as birthday's come and go, I wanna be
there
Celebrating with you, enjoying those times with you
As the years come and go and the seasons grow short,
I wanna be there to catch the last sunsets
When your hair is finally all grey and your heart beats come slower
I wanna be there to lay my head on your chest,
And listen to your heart slowly beat no more
As you walk upon the clouds, and sleep under stars
I wanna be there with you forever more

Tell Me What You See

You said that you see a dead end
That you can't see further
You looked into my eyes and asked, "Tell me what you see"
What I see, you may not believe
I see us walking down aisles hand in hand
I see us laughing and crying
I see us walking on secluded beaches
A breeze washing over us
I see us sleeping under stars, telling of dreams, wishes, and hopes
I see us fighting, arguing, and yelling
Yes, there will be tears, but I also see talking and making up
I see kisses under mistletoes, I see new years come and go
All with me and you
I see us with friends and family around celebrating and loving
I see when you and I are gray, me chasing you around to give you a
gummy kiss
Yes I can see all of this,
To me, this is true bliss
But if you can't see all of this, even if you close your eyes
I shall give you my eyes so you can see what my heart sees

I Want To Stay Lost

Far too many times have I taken
Times like these for granted
Wanting to rush, wanting to jump
Not taking the time to enjoy
The simplicity and joy that times like these can bring
Now I just want to get lost in this moment
I want to get lost in the feeling of your hair as it falls upon my shoulders
I just want to get lost in the moment of the way your skin
Feels under my finger tips, how soft it feels
The smell of your scent is like a fresh, cool breeze on a hot day
The light in your eyes, entices me, makes me want to get lost
Makes me lose track of time as I gaze into your eyes
The kiss from your lips is soft and sensual
I don't want to let go of our embrace
If by somehow, some way these times some how vanish as quickly as they
came, I will do whatever I can to be back in those moments
If some how I should fall and fail, I shall not be sad, I shall not regret
for even though I would still want to be in those moments forever more
At least I cherished the moments I had/have with you

I Would Get to you

I don't care how long it would take I would get to you
I would drive how ever long and rest along the way
but I would get to you
My love doesn't stop, not when I have to have you
I would get to you
I could sleep when I am next to you
I could sleep when I have you in my arms
No matter how, I would get to you somehow
My heart wouldn't rest until it was with you
I would get to you and sleep with you in my arms
I wouldn't stop until I was staring into your eyes
Kissing you smelling you loving you
Our hearts would be beating as one
I would get to you because my heart is with you

It Still Remembers You

It's been 6 years since we last touched

But yet my heart still can't forget that touch

Those eyes that lit up the room

Your skin felt so smooth next to me
the way you held me at night
felt so right

At times now it feels like a dream
like you didn't exist
but my heart still remembers you
At times even now I still hear your voice in the trees
when there is a slight breeze
At times even now your kiss can still be felt on my lips

I don't know how or why I fell in love with you
I just know that I did
I can't get you out of my head
No one else has hurt or touched me the way you have
I still hope that you were a dream but my heart still remembers

It still remembers not just how it ended
but the nights we had together
the times we spent together
it still remembers you

Just Another Face

I loved spending time with you
You were the only one that I could just sit and just be with
There could be no talking and it was fine
We could go out and have a great time
And that would be fine
You were special to me
But our time was short
Maybe it was me who turned my back first
Maybe it was you
But add that to the list
Like a record that kept playing
I tried asking you out again
But the excuses were many
And my phone never rang
I refused to chase again
Now as I look
My heart sees someone special
But my mind sees just another face

Walkin' You Slowly

―――❦❦❦―――

Somebody once told you that I was walkin' you slowly
I was walking with you slowly down this path
A path that we went down hand in hand
A Journey that we didn't know when it would end
I held you at night and woke up next to you when the sun rose
We spent time and troubles with each other
We told each other our fantasies and what troubled deep down in our
souls
We eventually stopped walking hand in hand
Eventually we stopped walking next to each other
I looked next to me and you weren't there
I looked behind and you took another path
I had hoped we would walk along this path together, longer than we did
As we go on separate paths
I miss those special times spent with you
This journey we take apart
Tugs relentlessly at my heart
Hopefully it will end with us back again on the same path hand in hand
But if we should never find ourselves walking side by side on the same
path
I will love you till this journey ends

Paralyzed

I didn't want to be wrong
I thought logic would make me strong
Instead I am weak
I hope to hear your voice
But I listen to nothing
I wait to see that smile that was so special to me
Hoping that the dysfunction that pervaded all throughout
Would last
And some how some way there would be another day
I don't know which way to go, hoping that we would find a way
I search for something to say
But I open my mouth and nothing comes out
I want to leave
I want to turn my back and walk away
But my feet wont move
My waist wont turn
I can only watch as you walk away
I can only see you smile, but not at me
I can only see you in some other's arms
But I can't move, I can't speak
Can't, wont get over it
Doesn't matter, because
I am paralyzed

 Today

Today I wanted to call
I just wanted to hear your voice like I used to everyday
Just to hear you say hi or I love you or anything else
At times I took it for granted that I could call I could hear your voice
Now its just another thing I miss
Today I wanted to eat lunch with you
Just to spend the precious few minutes with you
We used to rush and say, we had more time
Now there is no more time, there is no more tomorrow
Today I just want to hold you reach out to you
Keep your warm body next to me, to kiss you and hold you
I long for the days where we did nothing but be in the same room
Today I missed you more than the rest

The Journey

The journey to get here
has been rough
At times it has been tough

Wondering why hearts got broken
when they didn't need to be

Why couldn't they see
the pain they caused within thee?

Didn't they know
the love that was within
was all for them?

As I reach out for the one
my heart wanting, needing

Hoping I can hold you
Hoping I can kiss you
Hoping I can get lost
in this loving bliss again

The Future

As I look out from this cliff all I can see is clouds
I look behind and I can see the loves lost, and the hearts broken
I once thought that you were going to be here
At this cliff looking with me, straining to see our future
Now it's just me trying to see, trying to make something out
There are just clouds and fog
Despite that I try with everything to see something anything
I try to see you if you will come back or stay gone
Yet I can't even see the simplest thing
So I will just try and see
And hope you will be there

Tell Me

Tell me of your fantasies your dreams.
They will become my visions.

Tell me you're cold.
I will wrap my arms around you like a blanket.

Tell me you can't see.
My eyes will be your eyes.

Tell me you can't feel.
My fingers will be yours to feel with.

Tell me your heart can't feel.
I will give you my heart so you can feel.

If ever something hurts you
I shall shed a tear.

When you're happy
I shall smile with you.

If ever you have need for love
I shall love you until the end of time

Still

As our paths take us in different directions
I think of the times we spent
Laughing, loving, crying,
The places we have seen, and the things we have done
The life that we shared with each other
The love that came of it
As time went on love was the glue no matter the test
People came and went and I was still there
Maybe I should have been more patient maybe I should have done less
As the days that held you and I came and went my love
For you became stronger than anything, it was unbreakable
Now as the time between us grows from hours to days to months
My feelings for you are still as strong as the day we stopped talking
My unbreakable love for you is . . . . still unbreakable
I did love you unconditionally
I love you unconditionally now . . . . still

Standing On the Edge of Goodbye

Here I am standing on the edge of good bye
Knowing if I take another step we may never see each other again
We met and fell in love
We lost sight of our dream as time went by
That is why we are standing on the edge of goodbye

The look in your eye I will never forget
The kisses we shared will always be felt
The laughs that we had will always bring a smile
To get to our love it took a while
It only took one night to tear it apart
That is why we are standing on the edge of goodbye

When we made love it felt right
With a touch of your skin made my senses come alive
For a while our love did thrive
In the end words and actions tore away at our love
That is why we are standing on the edge of goodbye

Where ever we went people saw the love that we had right from the start
Some thought that we would never part
Now though every one wonders how we could have been torn apart
That is why we are standing on the edge of goodbye

Before I turn away I look the way you went
Hoping that you will come back my way
Believing that love will lead the way
For you should know that my love is true
I will always love you
Perhaps in another life we will find each other
But if we don't you will always have a special place in my heart
If we should meet in heaven
I will line a path of stars
So that you will find your way to me
For now we are standing on the edge of goodbye

Somewhere in the Middle

Back when this journey began I was floating on air
It was all I could do to not stare into your eyes
I knew that you missed me more than words
Just by the look that we shared
By just the touch of your hand I knew that you loved me
Though my ears were always filled with that sound
Never a night went by that I did not hear you say good night
I could see that smile that to me is sunshine on a cloudy day
I could hear that laugh that made my heart smile
We could barely get enough of each other
Yes, I know that it can't always be the same as the first time
But does it have to feel like the last time

Though, this feeling might be misplaced
I still can't help feeling that something has gone
Though I may not be able to pin it down
But I can describe it

It feels like waiting to hear a soothing melody but hearing nothing
It feels like walking on the hardest stone after you have been walking on air
It feels like you were important enough, but now somehow someway,
You have been set aside like an old hat
It feels like falling, and the sensation of no one there to catch you

I know it can't always be the same
I don't want to suffocate
But I don't want to be blown away by a breeze
I just want to be somewhere in the middle

𝔖𝔱𝔞𝔫𝔡 𝔑𝔞𝔨𝔢𝔡 𝔍𝔫 𝔣𝔯𝔬𝔫𝔱 𝔒𝔣 𝔈𝔞𝔠𝔥 𝔒𝔱𝔥𝔢𝔯

Let's discard all the façades that we put on for society
Take off all the clothes that we use to hide that
Which we don't want others to see
Take off shoes that sometimes get
Burden down with the hardships of life
Let your hair down
So you can be
Free in front of me
Nothing to hide
From each other
Can't keep anything from being seen
Let's stand naked in front of each other

Sit and Wonder

As I sit and wonder how it could end up this way
Was I so blind not to see
Was I so cold as not to be able to feel
Did I lose the fore sight not to be able to see what might have happened
For now you are no longer here with me
I no longer hear your voice
I no longer feel your loving touch
I no longer see your smile in front of me
As I sit and wonder how could it end up this way
The way we loved
The way we touched
The way we looked at each other
Now I just sit and wonder

Present from Santa

At times I am going to be gruff
Maybe the edges will be rough
True an asshole I can be
A little ditzy you may see
Forgetful it may seem
Even at times too quite
Or it may seem that I don't pay attention
But my love, you will never wonder where my love for you went
For in my heart you will always find thee
Like the great oak, it grew from an acorn into a mighty tree
My ears will always seek your words
My skin will always hunger for your touch
My heart will always be quenched by your love
For it is your love that I have sought
It is your love that this year Santa has brought

Passion's Poem

Once I put you up on a pedestal
So everyone could see
You were the one for me

There wasn't anything I wouldn't do for you
When times were tough I was there
Through any storm that was rough

Once you rested your weary head on my chest
Now you rest on a pillow

As we sit back and ponder
I wonder about the days spent together

Now as we look back upon the ruins
All the things that have been said and done
It's finished, before our lives together had begun

Now I ask
Will fate bring us back
Or will we travel different paths
Never to hold each other again?

Oh Sweet Dove

Oh sweet dove
come and tell me of my love.
Come whisper in my ear
Has she disappeared?

Will she reappear
Do I have reason for my fears
Are there going to be any tears

Oh sweet dove
Come and tell me of my love
My days are filled with thoughts of her

I can smell her sweet scent in the air
when others pass by

Oh sweet dove
Come and tell me of my love
Let me touch her
Caress her
Kiss her
Hold her

Oh sweet dove
Come and tell me of my love
Let me love her.

My Wish

This is my wish:
of the miles between us there be only one
If any at all

A wish from me to you:
that I just want to be next to you

A wish from my heart to yours:
that every day is filled with thoughts of you

A wish that is felt from head to toe:
that I only want to hold you more than you know

A wish that will show
how much you mean to me

A wish that I hope reaches the heavens above:
My thanks for you, the heaven-sent an angel
who I love

My Last Love

The journey to get to you

Has been tough

Many times it has been rough

Tears have fallen like rain

At times the heartbreaks were nothing but pain

At times I thought I had lost my way

I thought I was going to be eternally lost

Only to find my way again

I have touched and kissed

But never felt the way when our lips touched

When I went to bed at times I dreamt of you

I dreamt of my last love

One who would love me and make me whole

Now I can rest

Now I can breath

For I have found my last love

My Angel's Poem

Like a lone star in the sky
not alone, just outshines the rest
unique and special to my eye

Her beauty matched by no other
Her smile is the sun
Her eyes are the stars

Like a Dove
she is an angel sent from
heaven above

Like how the hands of time intertwine
I have only one question
how can I make her mine.

𝔜𝔬𝔲 𝔥𝔞𝔳𝔢

While the wind blows and chaos of the day goes on
It doesn't phase me cause there you will be
Your smile is what I live for
Your touch I can feel for hours and still want more
that is what I miss when I am at work
I think of making you happy with a word or a rose
there is nothing I wouldn't do for your love
I just want to love you. my heart is all for you
You have captured my smile with your laugh
You have made me feel loved with your touch
You have lit up my life with your smile
I just want to hold you all through the night
You have captured my soul with your heart

You Are The Reason I Live

You are the reason I live
Only to you my love I will give

In the morning when I wake
My body trembles I shake
With every thought of you

Maybe I don't know what love is
Buy I do know
You are truly sent from above
Because it's you I do truly love

Would You Believe That There Could Be A Man

Would you believe that there could be a man

Who could stand in the middle of a bar and his only thought would be

of you

He is not weak or ignorant

But strong and intelligent

Would you believe that their could be a man who would

Give his heart to you no matter if you loved him or not

For he realizes that when he met you his heart was not his

Would you believe that there could be a man who wants to be

Your rock, your pillow, your everything

Would you believe that there could be a man

who could feel complete when you are around, that believes that you are

the only he wants

Would you believe that this man exists?

He does, he is me.

Words Unsaid

These words may not ever grace your ears
I want to scream, yell, shout
I love you come to me
I want you to understand the pain
With the passion of these words
With the conviction of a thousand voices
Raising up to the heavens saying one thing
I love you
With the force of a tidal wave
That's how much I want you to stay
But with each passing hour of the days that go by
You will not hear these words
For these words are words unsaid

Why Must We Leave Like This

Why must we leave like this
Knowing that we still love each other
Knowing that we still want each other
Why must we leave like this
Still hopeing, believing that maybe one day
Why must we leave like this
Still hoping for one more day and one more night
Why must we leave like this
Our hearts were one, loved with no end
Why must we leave like this
Still wanting to be with each other
Why must we leave like this
Knowing that at night we miss each other the most
Why must we leave like this

When

When everything has been said
All the words spoken from your mind, body and spirit
All the things that could be done, have been done
All the arguments have been started and ended
All the words said in anger and pain have been uttered
When all the anger has been drained and the hurt has been felt
Is when love will rise
Is when all the tears will fall, like leaves in the fall
For all that is left is the love we shared

When Was The Last Time

When was the last time
you were held by someone
who was true?

When was the last time
you were told you were
the only one?

When was the last time
you were in love with someone
and they were in love with you?

If I was yours
the answer would be
everyday.

What's It Going To Be

Tis true that I don't have what you want
Right now
An apartment or a place of my own
I do not own
I do not have a job
Though I am striding
Toward that end
Yes it is true with my parents I do live
But I do not ask that you forgive
Because there is nothing to be ashamed
In the end
When I have the place of my own
To live, to be proud of
When I have a career to help provide
Where behind lies I do not have to hide
When I can stand proud
Instead of looking down upon me
What is it going to be

What I Want To Do

I just want to kiss your soft lips,
Hold you until the break of day,
Get lost in your eyes and
All that would matter would be you and I.

I want to be your friend, lover, companion,
Have you tell me what's in your heart,
What's on your mind and what's in your soul.

Hold your hand, take a walk, argue with you.
These are the things I want to do with you.

Watch you breath, make you happy, make you smile,
These are things I would live to do with you.

Come to me . . .
I will cherish you like a thirsty man
would cherish a glass of water in the desert.

Wanting More

When I gaze into your eyes I want to get lost in that moment
And not want to be found
I want to you hold you like the Sun holds the flower
Kissing your lips
Is Like kissing a single strand of silk
I want more
I listen to your voice and
I loose myself wanting to hear every word
Every detail
I wish there more hours in the day
Not to work nor to sleep, but to spend with you
I hungrily want more like the grass hungers for rain
I will take drops until I can feel it rain down upon me